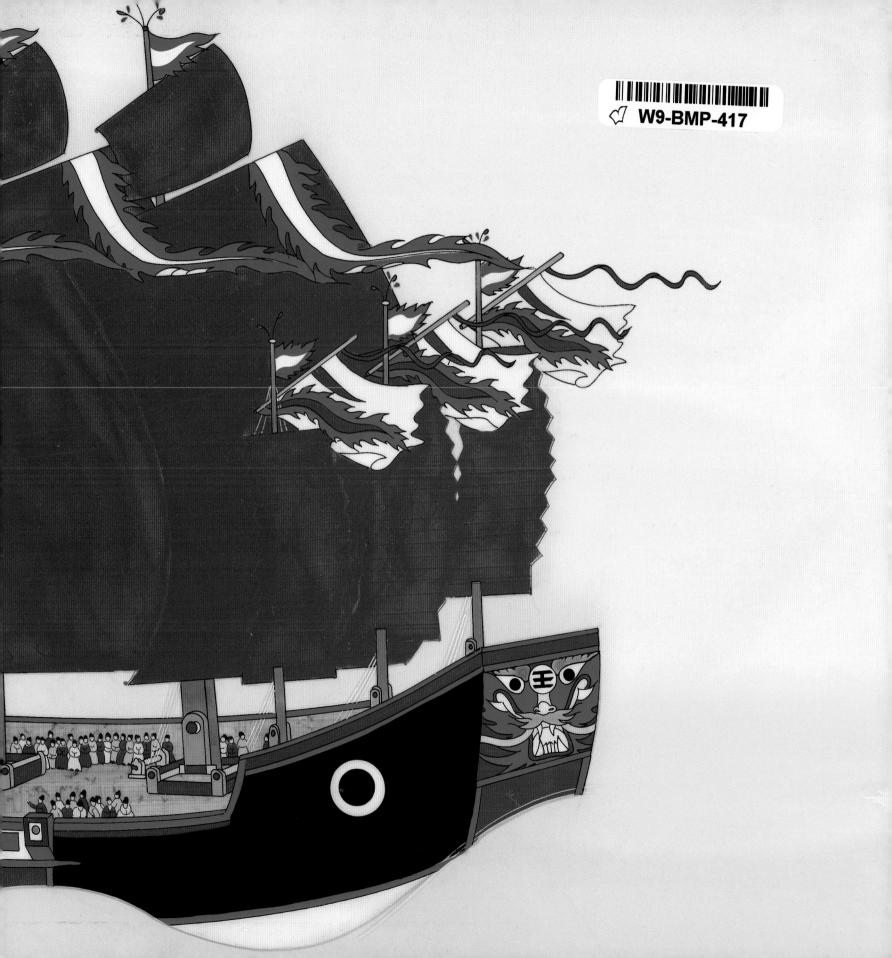

The Great Voyages of Zheng He

For great voyagers of all ages.

Shen's Books, an imprint of LEE & LOW BOOKS Inc.,
95 Madison Avenue, New York, NY 10016, leeandlow.com

Book design by Michael Nelson
Book production by The Kids at Our House
Manufactured in China by RR Donnelley
Printed on paper from responsible sources
10 9 8 7 6 5 4
First Edition

LIBRARY OF CONGRESS CATALOGING-IN-PUBLICATION DATA
Demi. The great voyages of Zheng He / by Demi. p. cm.
Audience: Grades 4–6. ISBN 978-1-885008-45-9 1. Zheng, He, 1371-1435—Travel—
Juvenile literature. 2. Explorers—China—Biography—Juvenile literature. I. Title.
DS753.6.C48D46 2012 951'.026092—dc23
[B] 2012000934

The Great Voyages of Zheng He

WRITTEN and ILLUSTRATED

by

DEMI

SHEN'S BOOKS, *an imprint of* LEE & LOW BOOKS INC., New York

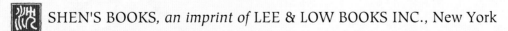

Zhu Di wanted the world to know of China's power, so he began building the largest navy the world had ever seen. He appointed Zheng He the Admiral of the Navy because of his integrity and his knowledge in warfare, and also because of his learning in the arts and religion.

He also expanded and repaired the Grand Canal, fought the Mongol raiders in the north, strengthened the Great Wall, and energized China into a superpower.

Emperor Zhu Di had big ideas.
He was a capable and ambitious ruler
who wanted the brilliant Ming Dynasty
to be the greatest and most powerful
of all. He expanded and rebuilt the
Forbidden City in Beijing.

Ma He's loyalty and skills had helped Zhu Di defeat his rivals. In gratitude, Emperor Zhu Di gave Ma He wealth, title, and the noble family name of Zheng He.

In 1402 Zhu Di gathered his forces and rebelled, deposing Zhu Yunwen and making himself emperor.

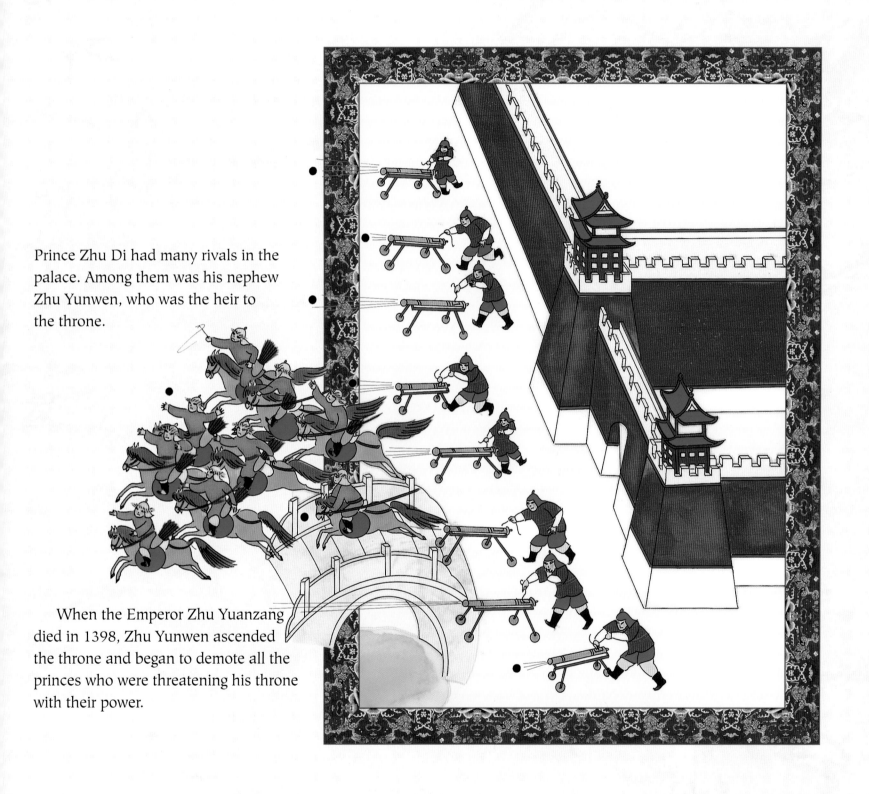

Prince Zhu Di had many rivals in the palace. Among them was his nephew Zhu Yunwen, who was the heir to the throne.

When the Emperor Zhu Yuanzang died in 1398, Zhu Yunwen ascended the throne and began to demote all the princes who were threatening his throne with their power.

Ma He was educated in the palace, and from the start distinguished himself in every subject and skill. He was so bright that the court nicknamed him *"San Bao,"* meaning "Three Treasures." When he grew older he proved so loyal and brave that Prince Zhu Di rewarded him with the power to plan military strategies.

When Ma He was ten years old,
the powerful Ming army defeated the
Mongol forces and captured Kunming.
Ma He's father was killed in battle,
and Ma He was brought to the
Imperial Palace in Nanjing to serve
the Prince Zhu Di.

IN 1371 a little boy named Ma He was born in Kunming, a city in the Chinese province of Yunnan. His family was Muslim and he had one brother and four sisters. Growing up, he heard stories of how his family had come from Bukhara, Persia, and how his great-great-grandfather had fought alongside the great Mongol ruler, Genghis Khan, and was made the governor of Yunnan province. He heard stories of his father's pilgrimage to the Holy Land of Mecca, and hoped to one day go there too. Ma He loved to read adventure stories. His favorite was "Sinbad the Sailor," which he read in Chinese and Arabic.

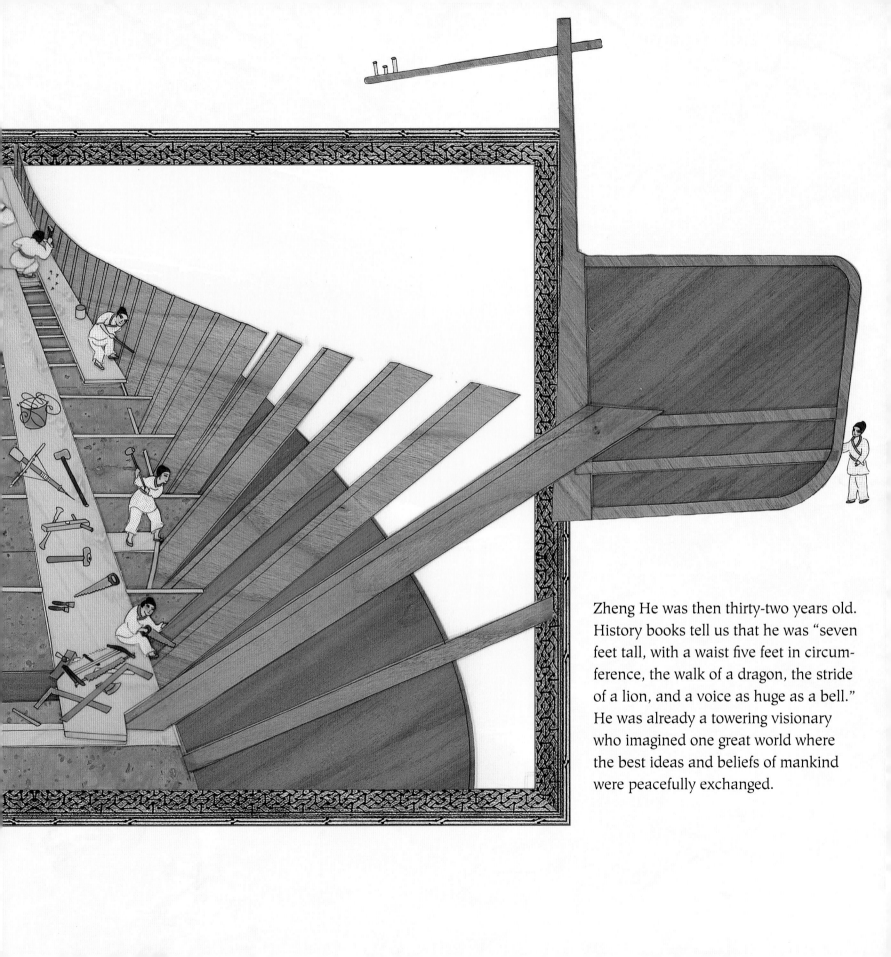

Zheng He was then thirty-two years old. History books tell us that he was "seven feet tall, with a waist five feet in circumference, the walk of a dragon, the stride of a lion, and a voice as huge as a bell." He was already a towering visionary who imagined one great world where the best ideas and beliefs of mankind were peacefully exchanged.

In 1403, Zheng He received orders from Emperor Zhu Di to build 525 ships. This was a mammoth undertaking involving supplies from the entire empire.

It took two years to build the sixty-two great "Treasure Ships." They were gargantuan: each was 400 feet long and 170 feet across, and had nine masts, twelve sails, a 50,000-square-foot main deck, a displacement of over 3,000 tons, and a hold for 15,000 tons of cargo. These ships were ten times the size of Portuguese explorer Vasco da Gama's flagship, and were the largest wooden ships ever built.

Escorting the Treasure Ships were the "Galloping-Horse Ships," the fastest in the fleet. They were 370 feet long and each sported eight masts. There were also 280-foot ships that carried supplies, 240-foot ships that carried troops, and 180-foot junks that were for combat.

Thirty thousand sailors and marines manned the ships, which also carried hundreds of Ming officials, 180 physicians, and countless sail makers, herbalists, blacksmiths, carpenters, tailors, accountants, merchants, and interpreters.

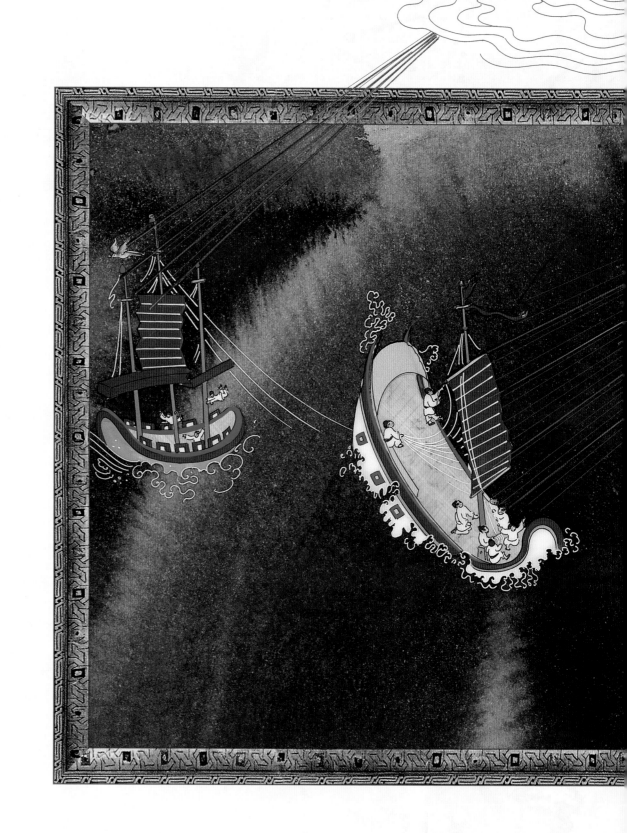

The Emperor and Zheng He prayed to the Buddhist goddess Bodhisattva Mazu, Protector of the Seas, for safe voyage. They built many temples to honor her. The most famous still stands in the Longjiang shipyard.

Zheng He wrote, "During the voyages, whenever the fleet met with thunderstorms at the high sea, a Goddess would appear in the clouds and a flash of red light like a ray of sunlight would fly toward the ships. Soon after, the stormy sea was as calm as before and the ships sailed safely."

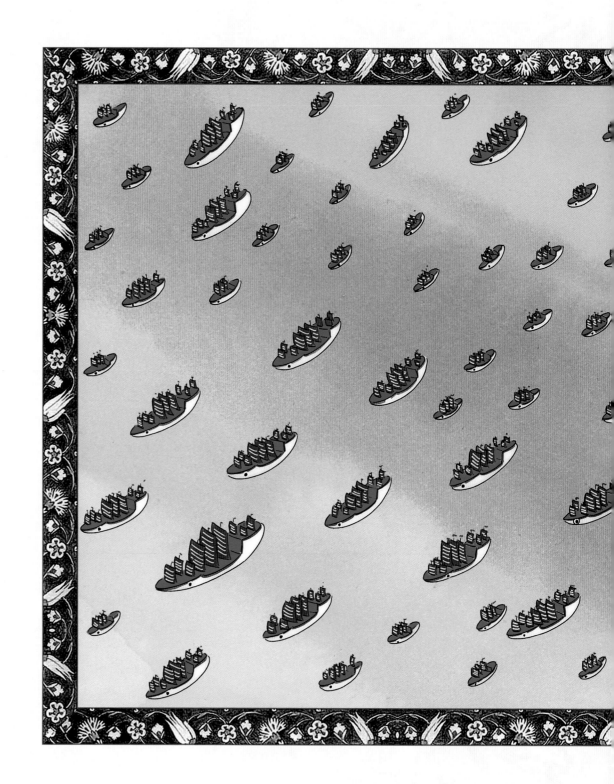

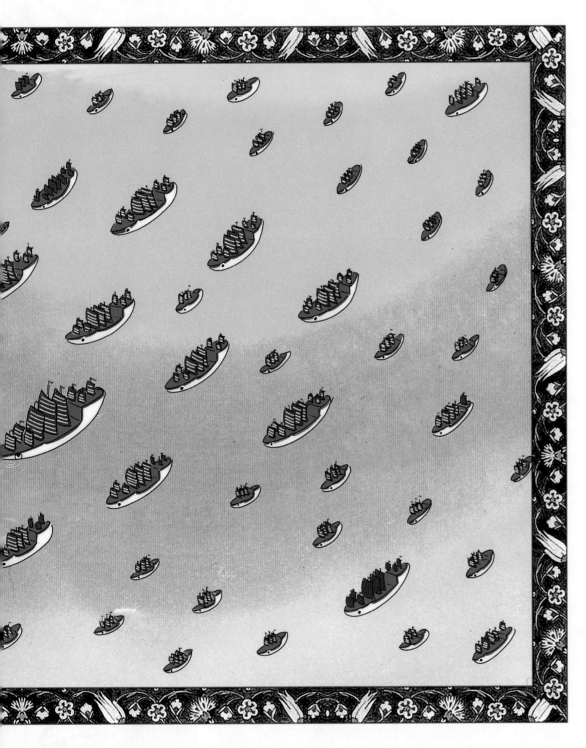

In 1405, Zheng He sailed out of Nanjing with the first 317 ships and 27,870 men.

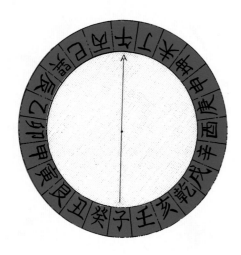

On this first voyage, Zheng He used a new, improved Chinese compass, new maps, and his knowledge of astronomy. He could calculate a ship's movement and direction on the vast ocean surface, and he could chart and follow a pre-determined route on the sea instead of following the coastline, where many ships wrecked.

The trade he carried was porcelain, silks, spices, cotton, brocades, iron, salt, tea, hemp, wine, oils, candles, and much, much more.

Zheng He's fleet sailed south to Champa, Java, and Sumatra. People everywhere were astounded at the approaching sight: stretching across miles of ocean, sailing straight toward them, were hundreds of ships, gigantic ships—cities of ships—with flaming red sails, dazzling in the sunlight! This was the terrifying majesty of Zheng He's armada, and everyone bowed before it. When the people saw the riches and beauty of the China trade, they wanted to be a part of it, and diplomatic relations were right away established with China.

Zheng He reached out with a policy of peace to all the rulers and people he met everywhere. When he saw the sick and the unfortunate, he automatically aided and protected them. By nature he was a brave, decisive, and noble man who was especially fond of doing good, so he was admired and respected wherever he went.

In the Strait of Malacca, Zheng He encountered the infamous Cantonese pirate fleet led by Chen Zuyi. In a fierce battle, the pirate fleet was completely destroyed and Chen Zuyi and five thousand of his pirates were killed.

Zheng He opened up the seas for peaceful trading.

Eventually, more than thirty foreign states would acknowledge Chinese supremacy, pay official visits to the Emperor of China, and bear tribute. In return for diplomatic recognition, they received military protection and trading rights.

Zheng He sailed to Ceylon and traded for rubies, deep blue sapphires, yellow oriental topaz, and pearls. While there, he saw the high mountain in the center of the island with a giant "footprint of the Buddha" on top. Muslims on the island said the footprint was Adam's, and Hindus said the footprint was Shiva's. Zheng He said "it was everyone's" because he believed in freedom of worship within and among all faiths, and he prayed with all for peace.

He then continued on to Quilon, Cochin, Calicut, and India, and quickly established diplomatic relations. Calicut was "the great country on the Western Ocean," and there Zheng He found many similarities with China. He respected its army, navy, and judicial system, and he admired the people's sense of beauty and accomplishments in all the arts and sciences. He traded goods and goodwill, and he returned home with ambassadors bearing messages from their kings and tribute for Emperor Zhu Di.

Emperor Zhu Di was well pleased with the tribute bearers who arrived bringing elephants, parrots, peacocks, king-fishers' feathers, hardwoods, incense, ivory, tin, and more. In return, Zhu Di gave them gold, Chinese court costumes, and fine writing materials.

He immediately ordered a second
voyage of the great Treasure Ships.
So in 1407, the foreign ambassadors
from Champa, Sumatra, and India were
returned to their homes and Zheng He
continued to expand the Ming Dynasty's
Indian Ocean trade links.

In 1409 Emperor Zhu Di ordered a third voyage. This time, when Zheng He sailed into Ceylon he encountered a civil war. Hindu Tamil forces and Muslims were fighting to overthrow the Buddhist Sinhalese King, Parakramabahu IV. Zheng He and his army routed the rebels and secured the rightful king's position. This was the only overseas land battle ever fought by a Chinese imperial army.

To keep the peace, Zheng He erected a giant triangular stone in the city's harbor of Galle. In words carved in Chinese, Tamil, and Persian, Zheng He addressed Buddha, Shiva, and Allah, offering thanks for their compassion and moral virtue, and seeking continued protection for his fleet. At this time, while the rest of the world was fighting in the names of Shiva, Allah, and Christ, Zheng He was far ahead of his time, proclaiming in every language religious tolerance and world peace.

After three successful voyages, Emperor Zhu Di had enough treasure to build a magnificent porcelain pagoda in Nanjing. Over a period of twenty years, the pagoda rose to nine stories and over 240 feet high. It was built of the finest white porcelain-glazed tiles in the world, and featured exquisitely carved porcelain figures and animals. One hundred fifty-two porcelain bells chimed in the wind, and the top of the pagoda was covered in gold leaf that shone in the sunlight.

The pagoda was the centerpiece of the Bao'en complex, which had more than twenty buildings and terraces, beautiful gardens, and exotic trees. It was considered one of the wonders of the world.

Zheng He embarked upon his fourth voyage in 1413, sailing as far as Arabia. On board was an imperial chronicler named Ma Huan. Along the way, Ma Huan recorded all the people and places the voyagers encountered, as well as their beliefs, customs, history, and geography. Exotic plants and animals were also recorded, such as the mouse deer in Ceylon and birds' nests in Borneo. Meteorologists recorded weather patterns and navigators charted unknown waters. Zheng He's ships were floating encyclopedias.

When Zheng He landed in Hormuz, he immediately felt at home because he shared the people's religious beliefs and admired their rich tradition of culture, commerce, and marine history. Hormuz was the hub of international trade on the Persian Gulf, and Zheng He was able to make fabulous trades for the world's most magnificent pearls from Bahrain, precious stones, coral, gold, silver, copper, iron, cinnabar, salt, lions, leopards, and Arabian horses.

At this moment, Chinese influence abroad was at its peak. All the important trading ports in the Indian Ocean and China Seas—from Korea, Japan, the Malay Archipelago, and India to the East African coast—were under Chinese influence. All recognized the power of the Dragon Throne, and all sent tribute to the Emperor. Precious ambergris used for medicine, cowrie shells, sapphires, rubies, oriental topaz, and Persian carpets filled the Forbidden City.

But of all these amazing treasures, the ones the Emperor liked best were a pair of Arabian eyeglasses and a giraffe from Malindi.

Zhu Di was completely delighted with his giraffe, for he considered it a *Qilin*—a legendary creature of good fortune that appeared only in the most auspicious times of great peace and prosperity. It did not eat meat and avoided stepping on any living thing, and was thus a symbol of greatness.

In 1417 Emperor Zhu Di ordered a fifth voyage of the Treasure Ships to explore the Arabian Peninsula and, for the first time, Africa. The fleet divided into smaller groups to make new discoveries: in Arabia the ships explored Dhofar, Aden, and Mecca; in East Africa they explored Mogadishu, Baraawe, and Malindi.

The African tribute consisted of daggers, spices, gemstones, ivory, rhinoceros horns, onyx, white pigeons, monkeys, ostriches, zebras, stallions, lions, leopards, and elephants.

Zhu Di now had so many exotic animals that he ordered the construction of an imperial garden to house all his creatures. This became China's first zoo.

In 1421, Zheng He continued his shuttle diplomacy with his sixth voyage, returning ambassadors to their homes and bringing new foreign dignitaries back to China. He explored a great deal more of Africa and expanded trade.

Meanwhile, Emperor Zhu Di celebrated the completion of the Forbidden City on New Year's Day. Thousands of foreign envoys, officials, military officers, and the great public gathered in Beijing. A parade of lucky giraffes was led before the city's gates. The future seemed to bring nothing but boundless prosperity, continuing voyages, and tribute bearers.

China had become the world's first superpower. Europe was still in the Dark Ages, and China was at its peak, tapping the riches of the entire globe.

But on May 9, 1421, lightning struck the three greatest halls of the Forbidden City, completely destroying them. Fire spread throughout Beijing, killing many people. Also that year, in Shandong and Hunan provinces, there were grain shortages and severe famines. Many people starved to death. In Fujian province there were epidemics that killed over 250,000 people.

In the south, a rebellion in Annam drained the Ming army and its resources. In the west, the Tartars raided China's border, and in the north the Oriats rebelled in Mongolia. Zhu Di suspended all future voyages of the Treasure Ships.

Emperor Zhu Di died on August 12, 1424, at the age of sixty-four. His son, Zhu Gaozhi, ascended to the Golden Throne. Zhu Gaozhi had no interest in the world beyond his own pleasures, and thought his father's projects extravagant. He declared, "All voyages of the Treasure Ships are to be stopped."

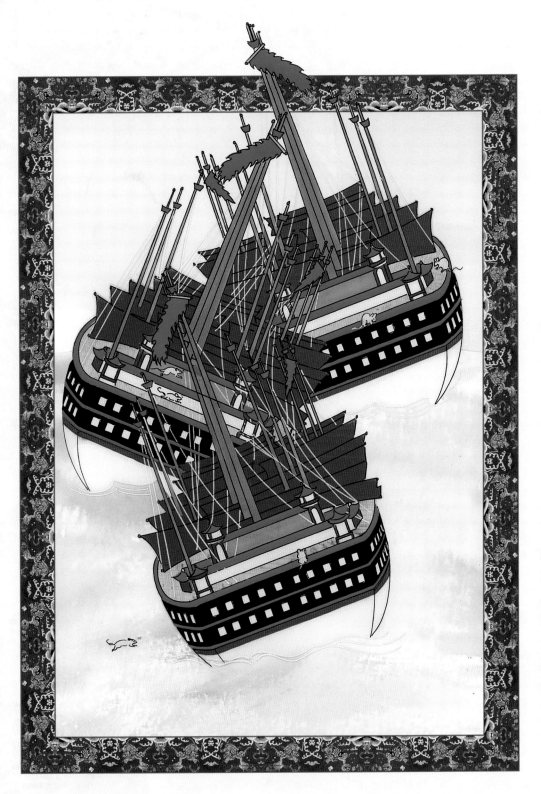

Zheng He was relieved of his duties as commander of the treasure fleet and put in charge of the military in Nanjing. The great ships were left to rot at their moorings and the records of their journeys were destroyed. All the great initiatives of Zhu Di were reversed. But on May 29, 1425, Emperor Zhu Gaozhi suddenly died.

Zhu Di's grandson Zhu Zhangji thus became Emperor. He wanted to re-establish the tribute trade in the Indian Ocean and make the "ten thousand countries our guests again." He immediately ordered a seventh voyage of the treasure fleet with Zheng He as commander.

And so Zheng He rebuilt the entire fleet.

The seventh voyage in 1431 was the largest expedition of all, with more than 350 ships and almost 28,000 men. It was a peacekeeping mission and the ships had names such as "Pure Harmony," "Lasting Tranquility," and "Kind Repose." Zheng He restored peaceful relations with Siam and Malacca, and sailed on to India, Mecca, and Jeddah, peacefully trading in every port. The ships went as far as the Swahili Coast of eastern Africa before returning home.

This moment was the peak of China's golden age of exploration. It seemed like a glorious dream to Zheng He, who said:

"We have beheld in the ocean huge waves like mountains rising sky high, hidden in a blue transparency of light vapors, while our sails, loftily unfurled like the clouds, day and night continued their course, rapid like that of a star, traversing those savage waves."

Returning home across the Indian Ocean, Zheng He suddenly died at the age of sixty-two. In keeping with the Muslim tradition, he was buried at sea with his head facing Mecca. His beloved sailors bid him a solemn farewell with Muslim prayers. His shoes and a braid of his hair were buried in a tomb in Nanjing.

The seventh voyage was the last great expedition of the treasure fleet. There was no man after Zheng He who had the knowledge or the skills to move China forward, outward, and into the world by sea. Within a few years, the greatest navy the world had ever known was extinct.

The legacy of Zheng He is as outsized as his ships. He was a man of towering ability, humility, compassion, brilliance and vision, whose mighty fleet reshaped an empire. His hundreds of ships spread Chinese culture from Indochina to Africa and perhaps even to Australia and the New World.

Zheng He dreamed of a world where the best of mankind was peacefully shared and celebrated, a world of intellectual growth and religious tolerance, and a world of everlasting, worldwide peace.

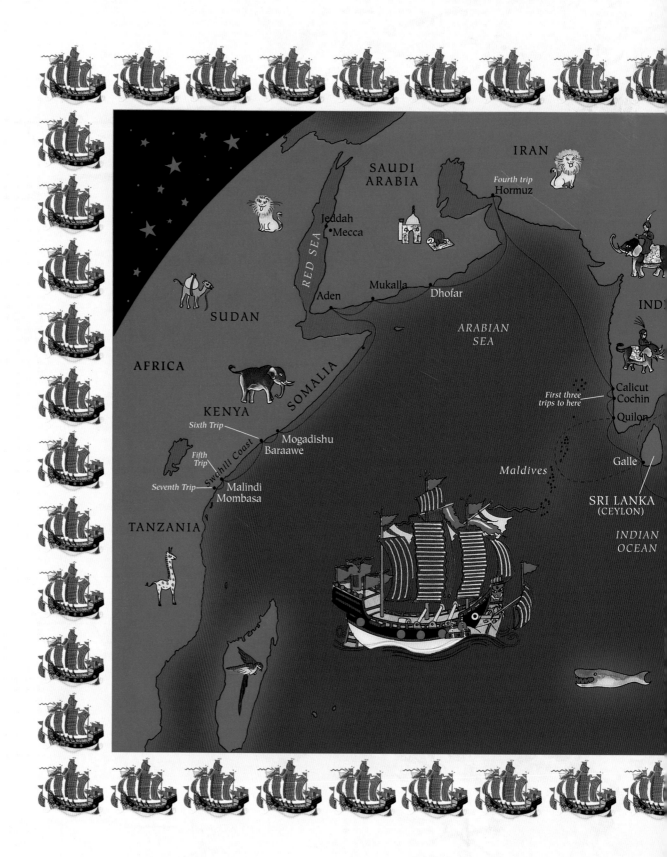

SAUDI
ARABIA

IRAN

Fourth trip
Hormuz

Jeddah
•Mecca

RED SEA

Mukalla

Dhofar

Aden

ARABIAN
SEA

SUDAN

AFRICA

INDI

SOMALIA

KENYA

Calicut
Cochin

*First three
trips to here*

Quilon

Sixth Trip

Mogadishu
Baraawe

*Fifth
Trip*

Swahili Coast

Maldives

Galle

Seventh Trip

Malindi
Mombasa

SRI LANKA
(CEYLON)

TANZANIA

INDIAN
OCEAN

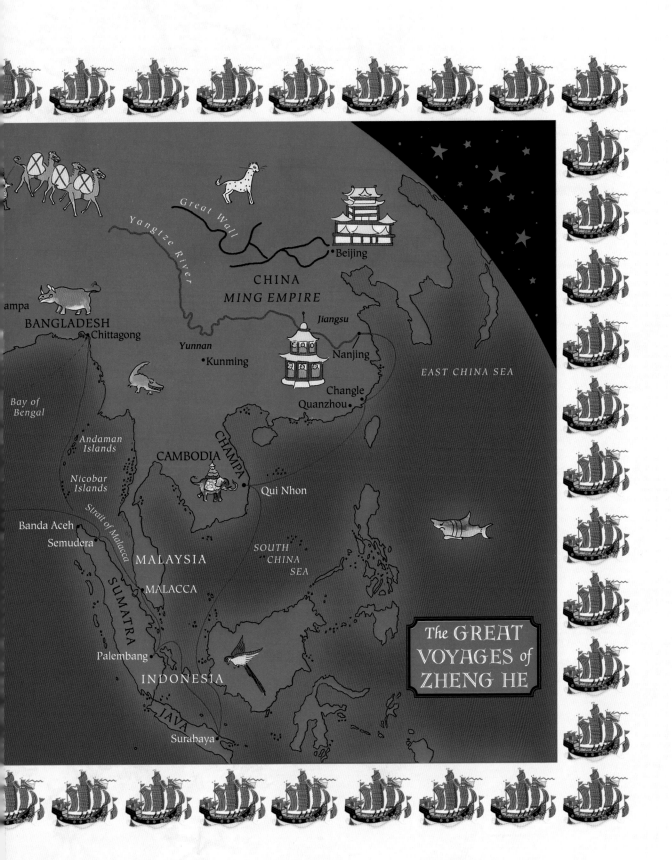

Great Wall

Yangtze River

CHINA
MING EMPIRE

Beijing

ampa

BANGLADESH
Chittagong

Yunnan
•Kunming

Jiangsu
Nanjing

EAST CHINA SEA

Changle
Quanzhou•

Bay of
Bengal

Andaman
Islands

CAMBODIA   CHAMPA

Nicobar
Islands

Qui Nhon

Banda Aceh

Strait of Malacca

Semudera

MALAYSIA

SOUTH
CHINA
SEA

MALACCA

Palembang•

INDONESIA

JAVA

Surabaya

The GREAT VOYAGES of ZHENG HE